Frank Lloyd Wright Home and Studio, Oak Park

Text
Elaine Harrington

Photographs
Hedrich-Blessing

Edition Axel Menges

Editor: Axel Menges

Published in cooperation with The Frank Lloyd Wright
Home and Studio Foundation.

© 1996 Edition Axel Menges, Stuttgart
ISBN 3-930698-23-4

Reproductions: Bild und Text GmbH Baun, Fellbach
Printing and binding: Daehan Printing & Publishing
Co., Ltd., Sungnam, Korea

Design: Axel Menges

Contents

Frank Lloyd Wright's Home and Studio in Oak Park

In 1889, Frank Lloyd Wright borrowed $ 5,000 from his employer, architect Louis H. Sullivan. He used this sum for a mortgage on a piece of property in Oak Park, Illinois, and to buy building materials to erect a small house there.[1] On 1 June 1889, he had married Catherine Tobin, a young woman from Chicago. Their honeymoon cottage grew in size and stature to accommodate the Wrights' family and his architectural practice, and along the way sparked an architectural movement centered in the midwest of the United States, known as the Prairie School. In 1976, this significant and unusual complex was named a National Historic Landmark.

Wright's building site, a tangle of plants and shrubs, was at the south-east corner of Forest Avenue and Chicago Avenue in Oak Park, which had developed as a suburb after 1871. It lies nine miles west of Chicago's Loop and was connected to the city by several train lines.[2] Wright bought the corner property, which measured 88 feet along Forest Avenue and 205 feet along Chicago Avenue, from landscape gardener John Blair, who had planted the lot with many specimen plants.[3] To this day, the massive ginkgo tree, now over a century old, continues to shade the rear courtyard by the studio.[4] Wright's mother, Anna, and his two sisters moved to the former Blair house, a small white Gothic Revival frame house with jig-sawn barge boards facing Chicago Avenue at the eastern end of the site. Wright built his own home closer to the corner of Forest Avenue.

Frank Lloyd and Catherine Wright started their family, which grew to six children. Twice Wright added onto his original honeymoon cottage of 1889. The first addition in 1895 was to accommodate this growing family. It included a new, larger dining room, a new kitchen and a children's playroom. This expansion enlarged the home to a total of 3,581 square feet. The second addition, of 1898, was the studio wing for his expanding architectural practice. It incorporated 2,596 square feet, which brought the entire building to a total of 6,177 square feet.

The original house was not modern but rather Victorian in character, and it also incorporated Wright's earliest architectural ideas. The building evolved in 1895 with more horizontal lines, more sophisticated art glass, recessed lighting and coordinated furnishings as he tried out his developing architectural vocabulary. The 1898 wing brought this pre-Prairie School work to a fuller realization as Wright explored spatial effects, experimented with restrained details, created purpose-made furnishings, and made a work place into an architectural statement.

Wright set his home well back on the lot, respecting the set-back line of other houses on Forest Avenue, a paved residential street. First impressions of the 1889 structure were of a simple, geometric, shingled house with a gable roof. The solid brick of the front veranda parapet gave privacy to family members as they sat on it in wicker rocking chairs. This terrace, as Wright called it, provided a platform from which to view the front lawn, and it visually anchored the house to the ground. Planters on both sides of the five steps up to its front entrance framed the front door. The first floor of the Forest Avenue façade is modulated by two an-gled bays, a treatment that is similar to one on a 1886 home by architect Bruce Price in Tuxedo Park, New York, published in an architectural journal before Wright built his home.[5] The Palladian window in the shingled second story gable of the façade, a feature of the house today, was actually one of many changes to the building initiated by Wright prior to 1909. The section immediately under the half-round lunette was part of the shingled wall as shown in historic photographs before 1895.

The entry hall of the home featured a painted plaster frieze in high relief of the *Battle of the Gods and Giants*, cast from the altar of Zeus at Pergamum. This had likely been purchased from the catalog of a source in Boston, the Caproni Company.[6] Diamond-paned casement windows introduced in the entry were carried through the 1889 portions of the home.[7] Originally the front stairway to the second floor from this hall was large-scaled with flowing bottom steps. Wright changed it to a narrower version before 1909.[8]

The living room, to the left and north of the entry, catalogs sources of design Wright employed in the early part of his career. The Colonial Revival for example is suggested in the diamond-paned glass in the windows and by the dentil moldings on the ceiling panels. The fireplace inglenook with its built-in benches on both sides is an element from the English Arts and Crafts movement. Open rectangular spaces above the benches on each side combine with a mirror over the oak-paneled chimney breast to give an illusion of depth of space. The arch of the fireplace opening is also found in the work of Wright's two employers, Joseph Lyman Silsbee and Louis Sullivan. Swirled foliate plaster panels in the ceiling and stencils on cupboard doors on either side of the family mottos over the fireplace are designs used in Adler and Sullivan's Auditorium Theatre and Hotel, the building Wright first worked on when hired by the firm.

The solid proportions of the walls in the room, and the way they are framed with woodwork, suggest movable fusama (Japanese opaque sliding panels). Initially the room had only one bay window. It overlooked the open front veranda on the west. The second bay window was added into the wall of the roofed side veranda on the north in about 1895. This pair of windows is early evidence of Wright's career-long fascination with windows that meet in a corner. This combination is similar to the corner window configuration shown in the floor plan in an illustration of the same Tuxedo Park house that Bruce Price published in 1886.[9] Wright could have also noticed a similar corner in the Tacoma building by Holabird and Roche, completed in 1889 in Chicago. The built-in seats under the bay windows made a sofa unnecessary in the room.

Behind the living room on the north-east side of the house was a room used originally as a dining room and later as a study. It was furnished with a built-in oak buffet and a china closet with a pass-through to the original kitchen which was to the south. After 1895, this room became a home study in which the Wright children did their schoolwork. It was from this study that Wright added a Japanese influenced passageway, which incorporated a tree within it, to connect the home to the later studio wing in 1898.

The larger, later dining room was created in 1895 from the original kitchen and a bay-windowed addition

1. Bruce Price, cottage in Tuxedo Park, New York. (From: *Building. A Journal of Architecture*, 18 September 1886; The Art Institute of Chicago)

2. The home from Forest Avenue, c. 1890–95. (Photographer unknown; published in: Henry-Russell Hitchcock, *In the Nature of Materials*, 1942; The Frank Lloyd Wright Home and Studio Foundation)

on the south side of the house. This room is the first Wright accomplished in which all parts were created as a whole composition: walls and floor, built-in display shelves, and free-standing furniture. The ceiling was dropped, and recessed lighting in a ceiling panel took advantage of the newly available technology of electricity. Art-glass windows demonstrated the architect's knowledge of design publications of the day, using a similar pattern published in a German art glass journal in Berlin in 1886.[10] After the house next door was built in 1897, the lower portions of the three central windows of this bay were filled in with panels for privacy.[11]

After the additions Wright created in 1895, the first floor rooms also included a pantry reserved from the first kitchen, a back stair, a servants' room, a kitchen hall and a new kitchen on the back of the original house. A black iron cook stove in the kitchen and a wooden ice box in the hall next to the kitchen door were the labor-saving devices for the cook. The family usually had two live-in servants, a maid who cooked and a stable hand. The washing woman came by the day to help.[12]

In the first scheme of the home, Wright placed a large studio for himself on the second floor across the front. Its oak floor had a stenciled border, evidences of which may still be seen around the perimeter of the room. After 1893, when Wright left Adler and Sullivan and took an office in the Loop, he remade this space into two children's bedrooms. The south half was the room shared by Wright's daughters, Catherine and Frances. His two younger sons, David and Llewellyn, shared the northern room. The two older boys, Lloyd and John Lloyd, were usually in Wisconsin at the school run by Wright's aunts, or at work on his uncles' farms.[13] The partition installed in the middle of the two rooms does not reach the ceiling, providing both air circulation and a more spacious effect to these bedrooms than if it extended the full height. Cupboards were added on the north and south when the room became bedrooms.[14] The boys' room communicated to the master bedroom through a closet.

The master bedroom located over the home study, or original dining room, featured a frieze decorated with a gold repeated stencil used in the Auditorium Theatre building. Murals of Native Americans were painted on the two end walls by Orlando Giannini, a muralist, illustrator and art glass designer often associated with Wright on architectural work. Glass double doors under a wood display shelf opened onto a narrow shingled balcony on the home's north side. The room's arched ceiling assisted in making it appear larger than its actual size.

The bathroom, entered both from master bedroom and the hall, featured handsome horizontal board-and-batten paneling, replaced as part of restorations to the building. Its corner window was reconfigured as part of remodeling in 1895, when the children's playroom was added.

On the south side of the hall Catherine Wright sewed and read to the children in the large room that was the result of the 1895 expansion of the early nursery into a day room, over the dining room. The room was adjacent to the back stair from the kitchen, had two built-in cupboards, on the west and east sides, the latter enclosing a sink, and functioned as a children's sick-room. The family's telephone was located just outside the day room on a wall of the hall. After

the house next door was built, the central panel of three diamond-paned windows at the bay end was filled in for privacy. A clerestory window facing south, with ecru art glass, gave additional filtered light to the space.

A hall with a low-arched ceiling led to the children's playroom added in 1895. The playroom with interior walls of Roman brick was large enough to be the setting for the children's dramatics and their play with dolls and Froebel blocks, the family's tall Christmas tree, as well as Catherine Wright's neighborhood kindergarten.[15] A shelf for toy and art display ran around the top of the room. The mural over the large fireplace in the east wall depicted the fairy tale from the *Arabian Nights* of *The Fisherman and the Genie*. The bay windows on the long sides of the room had leaded glass with geometrized flower designs, and toy-storage bins below. A concert parlor grand piano was suspended over the back stair from a steel strap still in place when restoration was started in 1974. Also over this back stair and the piano was a small stair up to the tiered, balustraded balcony, used alternatively as a stage or as audience seating for the children's play-acting.[16]

The visitor entered Wright's studio complex from Chicago Avenue, not yet paved when the building was first completed. The indirect path of approach from either side of a wall was created by 1909, by filling in the original wide steps up from the sidewalk. This provided an opportunity to view the two male sculptures on the roof called *The Boulders* and the plaster panels of storks in relief that guarded the windows of the loggia entrance porch. These sculptures were done for the building by sculptor Richard Bock who was associated with Wright on other commissions. In the reception hall, one's first impression is of golden walls and of dapples of sunlight by day or artificial light by evening illuminating its art-glass ceiling panel. Wright's business office was straight ahead, behind this hall. It had another art-glass ceiling panel, a round arched fireplace of common brick and a display shelf high on the walls on three sides of the room. The office was the location for the studio's telephone, desk and files.

To the left of the front reception hall, the large drafting room communicated with the office and the passage to the home. On the south side of the drafting room a vault supplied safe storage for the firm's architectural drawings, and especially for Wright's collection of Japanese prints. Square on the ground floor, the space became octagonal at the second floor level, which was a balcony suspended by chains from the roof, which was held in tension by an octagonal chain ring. Balcony windows were diamond-paned at first. These were later each one pane of glass within a frame of smaller leaded rectangles, with added clerestory windows above them.[17]

The later deck shelf that runs at balcony floor height around its opening was used to store plaster architectural models and sculpture. Photographs were processed in a sink at the top of the balcony stair above the vault on the south side of the drafting room. A quotation from Rudyard Kipling's poem »McAndrew's Hymn« of 1893, which had appeared in Scribner's magazine, used like a motto on the balcony wall set the theme of the room. The high windows gave daylight to the work at hand and when it was done, the large arched brick fireplace was used for clam bakes for drafting assistants and family too. The largest room in the building, the drafting room, was the setting for the marriages of Wright's two sisters, Jane and Maginel, when it was profusely decorated in daisies and black-eyed susans and autumn leaves.[18] For a time Maginel, an art student and later an illustrator of children's books, maintained a drawing table on the balcony, usually the work space of sculptors and art glass designers.[19]

From the reception hall a right turn toward a short windowless hall brought the client to Wright's own architectural library, an octagon in rotation of woodwork and wall. A skylight directed good light into the room. The library originally had diamond-paned windows as shown in historic photographs. These were later replaced with larger panes of glass in leaded glass frames like those of the drafting room. Tree tops could be seen through these high windows, but no other distracting view. Cupboards below shelves and windows in the library were for books and architectural plans on racks. In front of these cupboards were swinging cork panels upon which drawings could be pinned.

Wright decorated the studio with Arts and Crafts ceramics from the Teco Company of Illinois on many of the open shelves of both the drafting room and the library, which also displayed figurines, Japanese ceramics and prints, and a profusion of pine or leafy boughs. All parts of the room and its appointments were focused on the artistic atmosphere created by the architect's decorative collections and, most importantly, on presenting his work to prospective clients.[20]

Constantly throughout his tenure of both his home and its attached work place Wright made architectural changes to walls, windows and spaces, trying out his ideas. At least annually, and frequently more often, he rearranged and changed the rooms. Indeed, Wright's home and studio formed an architectural laboratory for him, and many of the designs created for it would find further refinement in commissions for clients.[21] The changes were documented in the numbers of photographs taken of the home and studio, many it is believed by the architect himself. Wright used an 8-by-10 plate camera and did his own developing.[22] In the 1890s he also photographed weeds and plants. He published some of these images and others he printed on Japanese tissue for his own use.

The architect's early life and career were inextricably part of this building. The complex that took shape in Oak Park was Wright's family's home, his office and the unfolding statement of his personal architecture. Wright brought his considerable creative energies to both the building and his use of it. The complex allowed his ideas to bear fruit, as he developed them through the many changes he made. At any time between 1889 and 1909 and after, this home and studio indicated his progress as a maturing architect.

The award-winning restoration of the structure began in 1974, with much of the work completed by 1987. In the home much original fabric survived to be restored, while in the studio many surfaces needed to be reproduced. The completed work presents the building as accurate to the Wright family's time and as the product of careful research within the building itself, interviews with surviving family members, archival documentation, and color and material analysis. It was restored to its appearance of about 1909, the

last year Wright actually worked in the studio, incorporating the many changes he had made up to that point, but returning the many changes he made after then to the targeted time frame. Understanding that any work on the building would destroy fabric designed by Wright at one point or another, the restoration team made a great effort to document its work. This documentation and parts removed from the building, such as plaster and paint samples, woodwork, bricks and art-glass windows, were carefully saved for any desired future research.

Wright was born in 1867 in Richland Center, Wisconsin and died in 1959 in Phoenix, Arizona. Even though he spent his early years in Rhode Island and Massachusetts, he is thought of as a midwesterner. He lived from 1878 in Wisconsin where he attended public schools in Madison. He entered the University of Wisconsin in 1886, where he studied civil engineering with Allan D. Conover but did not receive a degree. In 1887, he traveled to Chicago to seek work with an architectural firm. He was employed first in Joseph Lyman Silsbee's office to 1889, and then with Adler and Sullivan from 1889 to 1893.[23]

Wright and his wife Catherine Tobin Wright (1871 to 1959), from the Kenwood neighborhood near Hyde Park on the south side of Chicago, were young when they married at ages twenty-two and eighteen. Their youthful tastes and formative interests in music and art may have helped them plan their home. They went sketching together during their courtship and often chose domestic subjects. Wright's drawings of shingled houses, wild flowers and an elegant folded umbrella were more assured than Catherine's sketched plants and flowers.[24]

Catherine was likely to have learned something about home furnishing fabrics and colors through the position of her father, Samuel Tobin, manager of the upholstery department for a prominent Chicago dry goods firm, Farwell's.[25] She sewed and enjoyed making small gifts of needle cases, pen wipers, sachets, and pin cushions, from his outdated sample books.[26] Wright was already a keen observer of buildings, interiors and their decoration, beginning with the simple surroundings his mother had arranged when he was a youth.[27]

The larger portion of Silsbee's Chicago office production was in residential design, and in Adler and Sullivan's firm Wright was asked to work on the residential projects in the office, because both partners were busy with their larger commissions. These experiences helped to focus his thinking at this early time in his career on residential architecture. With his house, Wright could put into three dimensions his evolving beliefs about making a beautiful, eye-arresting, tasteful and functional home, a place for art and music, and for rearing children with spaces for their education and play. While his solutions may have varied, these were the same problems he addressed in his later career in other residential work, for example in the Prairie School, California textile block residences and the introduction of Usonian houses.

Wright's new home stood out from its neighbors. It presented an accentuated roof gable to the street, but was without the decorations of applied carvings, shutters and towers of most Oak Park houses of the 1880s. After the studio was added, the building was known locally as the house with a tree through it, be-

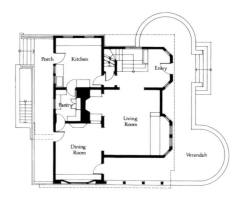

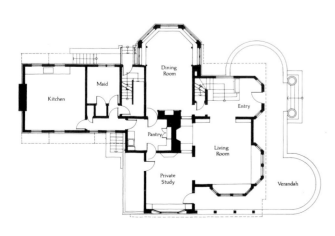

cause of the willow whose branches were preserved by having them emerge through the roof.

The studio made a statement about a working environment that was home-like in feeling, spacious, open, geometric, lit from a variety of handsome and technologically innovative sources, and decorated in an individualistic manner. With Wright's stone architectural sign embedded in the wall near the studio entrance, the whole building became an advertisement for his work.

Wright was interested in nature, the out-of-doors and the interaction of residence and site. He provided a fine view of the front yard from the house, and access from the original dining room to the roofed side veranda. The backyard included a walk past the ginkgo tree to his mother's house, with its gardens planted with typical varieties of perennials and shrubs, violets, wild ginger, lilies of the valley, snowball bushes, spirea, and lilac.[28] Wright was already using nature as an example of his thinking about organic architecture, where a design is harmonious with itself, its parts consistent with the whole.

Just as Wright considered and developed spaces for living and working, he also carefully and experimentally chose the colors for this building. The exterior shingles on the home and studio were initially stained medium brown. Later, before 1911, he put a green stain over the brown on the studio.[29] Wright employed the green colors of forests and the tawny shades of fields for the interiors. Two greens on the rough plaster walls and a lighter green on the frieze and ceiling in the entry hall and living room set the home's theme for family and visitors. The first dining room, later home study, had walls of green originally overlaid with a gold pattern. Nature's hues were continued in the ocher-toned burlap that covered the walls in the new dining room of 1895, in the painted warm gold walls of the master bedroom. The deep red tones of the second floor studio were changed to warm brown walls in the children's bedrooms. The Roman brick walls of the children's playroom were russet and its barrel-vaulted ceiling was ocher brown. The fresh light green walls of the early nursery with their silver stenciled frieze were changed to the more modern artist's canvas coverings, when the room was expanded to become Catherine's day room in 1895. The plaster kitchen walls were originally tan and by 1909 were painted a functional gray.

The studio drafting room was originally a reddish brown and later an ocher brown, as was the office. The studio reception hall, originally a rich deep red, and the octagonal library, originally olive green, both later featured gold toned walls painted in metallic powders to achieve an inviting and elegant Japanesque effect.[30]

Wall colors harmonized with the woodwork. In most of the rooms of the home the trim and built-in pieces were of oak. In the kitchen the trim was of pine and in the studio it was basswood. Floors in the home were of oak, except in the kitchen and bathroom where they were maple, and in the master bedroom which had a basswood floor and birch woodwork. Wright changed the studio's original wood floor to a uniform surface of magnasite, a blend of magnesium oxichloric cement and sawdust finished with linseed oil. With use it became a rich brown with a leathery appearance.[31]

In addition to its warm wood tones and wall colors from nature, this modest house and attached work place were enriched with displays of the family's art collections. Two works on the walls of the living room reinforced the artistic character of the house. A shady landscape oil by William Wendt, a contemporary Chicago artist, was balanced by a sunny farm field in pastels by Charles Corwin, the artist brother of Cecil Corwin, an architectural colleague of Wright's. Wright provided gold colored oak frames for these. Other art work included a print of a scene by Fritz Thaulov, the Norwegian impressionist, who exhibited at the 1893 Chicago World's Fair, and, in the children's playroom, a print of English artist Sir Lawrence Alma-Tadema's painting of *Reading from Homer*. A tempera by Orlando Giannini, who did murals for the house, and an oil painting of a forest view by Ernest Albert were in the family's collection, as was an oil of a pond and meadow by Charles Francis Browne, an instructor at the Art Institute of Chicago, where Catherine took art classes.[32] Catherine encouraged her children in their own artistic efforts. Japanese prints and paper stencils originally used in Japan for printing on fabric were given to them to play with, and they were encouraged to make home-made gifts for family members.[33]

Sculpture in the home included a copy of one of Hermon Atkins MacNeil's Native American pieces, *Navaho Orator*. Wright purchased many plaster copies of classical sculpture from the Caproni Company of Boston. He noted that the *Venus de Milo* and the *Winged Victory* were his favorite sculptures.[34] Two sizes of the Venus appear in historic photographs of his home and a large version of it was in the drafting room. The *Winged Victory* was over the entrance to the children's playroom which also had a plaster bust of the Venus on the mantel and a *Fighting Gladiator* on a shelf near the fireplace.[35]

In the studio the drafting room had a plaster copy of the bust called the *Psyche of Naples* on the deck shelf by the Kipling quotation, and a small copy of Michelangelo's *Dying Slave* was near the fireplace. It also had a plaster cast of the exterior decorative frieze of Wright's Heller House of 1896 over the fireplace.[36] A showpiece in the office at the end of the desk was the large plaque copy of Luca Della Robbia's *Boys Singing from a Book* from the choir balcony of the cathedral in Florence.

A bronze bust of Beethoven in the Wrights' living room is a reminder that this was a musical household in which all of the children were encouraged to learn an instrument. Both the piano and the Cecelian piano player in the playroom were used by family and drafting assistants alike.[37]

In addition to purchased furnishings for the building, Wright created specialized furniture for it. Wright was not the first American architect to design furniture for his interiors. Thomas Jefferson, Benjamin Henry Latrobe, Henry Hobson Richardson, and in Chicago, William LeBaron Jenney and Peter Bonnet Wight, were among those who had designed pieces that related to their interiors. However, he was one of the first young American architects to rethink the concept of furnishings that harmonize with their interiors and that are designed at the same time as the room in which they will be used. This approach became an integral part of Wright's work, and during his career he became noted for his unified interiors. He was evolving this

9

philosophy while in residence in Oak Park. Therefore, his earliest efforts in furniture design for his own home and for early clients were less related to the rooms they were intended to occupy than was characteristic of his career as a whole.

Two early oak armchairs created for his family in c. 1893, with cushioned high backs and seats of brown velvet and concave square spindles in the arms, demonstrate his observation of similar chairs by William Morris, adjustable back wood arm chairs that were likely exhibited and available for sale in Chicago.[38] These are also related to various designs by Henry Hobson Richardson for fixed back library armchairs that were published in 1888.[39]

When Wright added his home's new dining room in 1895, he used the opportunity to create a room that was all of a piece, with horizontal proportions in counterpoint to the tall dining chairs he designed at the same time. The straight backs of these seminal pieces, the first of his distinguished tall-backed dining chairs, framed the faces of the sitters in warm oak. When all were pulled up to the table, they created the feeling of a second, inner space within the dining room.[40] These chairs originally had spiral spindles in the backs and all the legs were straight. The backs later had square spindles installed to be more comfortable and the back legs were reworked to have a flare to improve their stability. Wright later had made an oak high chair for his youngest son, Llewellyn, to match the room.[41]

Wright created a deceptively simple chair for the cafeteria of the headquarters building he executed for the Larkin Company in 1903. With a one-piece back of a slanting board, the correct angle of which determines the comfort of the chair, this slant-backed chair is seen in many of his commissions, and a number were also in his own residence.[42] For the bedrooms he also designed various single, double and three-quarter beds.

As his early interest in Japanese prints grew, in about 1902, he planned several small foldable library tables for sorting and viewing them. These elegantly functional print tables had two drop leaves that each opened independently onto pairs of square spindled supports. They could be used as small library tables with one or both ends opened flat or both ends could be turned up like a big portfolio to make a narrow piece to store artistically against a wall. The one in the living room today is one of two Wright planned for his complex and is probably of yellow birch.[43] Print tables in oak were created for clients.

For the studio Wright designed a low-backed, square spindled armchair, one with lower proportions than the earlier ones used in the living room. The lower dimensions of the later chair design were in keeping with the noticeably horizontal lines of the studio. Although Wright's first Prairie School home was not designed until 1900, he clearly was experimenting with its horizontal proportions in 1898 i n his own studio and its furnishings. A very functional piece was the drafting stool that coordinated with the maple-topped oak drafting tables. One of them featured a gently slanted seat board, ergonomically designed to be helpful to the drafting assistants as they leaned forward over their drawings.

Foursquare wood chairs that Wright designed for the studio's office may have been inspired by a carved Chinese chair that he used in his living room in 1895/1896 according to photographs. The arms and especially the low cross braces of these chairs suggest an oriental source. These were without upholstery and were made more comfortable with cushions and leather skins.

In the 1890s Wright also designed decorative metal accessories for both his own home and those of clients. These became icons for this period of his work and included a tall copper weed holder and round urn for natural arrangements of grasses and boughs displayed in both the dining room and octagonal library.[44]

Wright designed lighting for many of the spaces in the building. Especially notable were the recessed ceiling panels that illuminated the dining room, where the electric lights behind quatrefoil fretwork took advantage of this new technology with eye-catching effect. The playroom featured both electric lights and skylights behind a fretwork that dramatically showed the leaves of the prickly ash in a conventionalized design. In the studio reception hall the skylight and electric lights above the art-glass lay light with its mellow colors made a pattern of green geometric leaves and golden pieces of sun overhead. A related lay light with art-glass accents in the office and the frosted glass of the octagonal library both had skylights over them that were also lit by electricity. The geometric pattern of the art-glass windows in the office was similar to that of its lay light.

The Wright home was wired for electricity in about 1891 some two years after it was built.[45] Wright was intrigued with this new convenience and did not believe that all the wires involved needed to be hidden in his experiments with fixtures. In the master bedroom pendant glass shades hanging from lotus flower decorated metal ceiling escutcheon plates in front of the murals became part of the wall composition. Historic photographs showed that over the balcony in the children's playroom striped optic glass globed lamps were clustered like a bunch of balloons. The wall sconces in this room integrated electric illumination within planar sheets of gold-tone art glass and an architectural framework of oak, designed after he had been in Japan in 1905 and demonstrating the influence of Japanese design.

In the studio drafting room prismatic Holophane-globed general lighting and adjustable individual lights hung from their electric cords, one green shaded lamp over each drafting table. Similar green shaded lamps were used in the office and were hung around the perimeter of the octagonal library.[46]

The house was originally heated with gravity fed hot air, but hot water heat radiators were introduced in the parts added starting in 1895, for example, at the window ends of the dining room and the day room above it and in the studio. In 1901 the Yaryan community hot water heating system was started in Oak Park and the Wrights' home was connected to it.[47]

Wright looked to built-in furnishings both to carry his architectural message and to provide functional storage for his family and clients. In his autobiography he noted, »Furniture and furnishings that were not built in as integral features of the building should be designed as attributes of whatever furniture was built in and should be seen as a minor part of the building itself even if detached.«[48] In his Oak Park home most

of the built-ins were of oak. The living room featured cushioned benches on both sides of the inglenook fireplace. This concept of built-in seating by a living-room fireplace was one he would return to in other work.

In the home's first dining room a long buffet under the window and a china cupboard accessible from front and back were built in. In the larger, more artistic dining room addition built-in ledges under the windows and over radiators supplied serving and display spaces. In the kitchen two kitchen counters over wood base cabinets on either side of the sink were provided as part of the restoration.[49] A closet and cupboards with glass doors above and drawers below were built into the master bedroom. When Wright converted his second floor home office into two children's bedrooms after 1893, a wall of wardrobes was added to each room.[50] In the playroom window seats in the bays incorporated storage with drop-front-opening spaces.

Basswood built-ins in the studio drafting room included open shelves at the windows over the radiators. High shelves on both sides of the fireplace and a linear deck shelf system added later afforded space for art objects and architectural models. The functional, built-in plan desk in the reception hall on which large drawings and plans could be spread for review with contractors, the cupboards in the small hall to the library that stored sample building materials, and cupboards for plans in the library were necessary to Wright's architectural practice. These were all stained a medium dark brown.

The family purchased ordinary furnishings and household items from other sources. Wright liked seeing how the rooms in his home looked with the furniture shifted around. When newly married, he attended house auctions and enjoyed placing his finds. For example, a blanket chest with early American or English carvings is shown in different rooms in historic photographs of the home.[51] This early learning process of improving interiors by moving pieces of furniture set a pattern for Wright of a lifetime of interest in furnishings and experimentation with their placement. A small carved teak taboret that the family used in different places in their living room may have shown Wright how handy a small stool or table could be. He designed them to the end of his career.

The Wright family purchased new items for their home from Marshall Field and Company department store and the Sears Roebuck Company, just as many other Chicago residents did. The family's good china, a white Limoges set with small gold details around the rims, came from Field's.[52] These pieces, and the family's everyday china of Blue Willow ware, were set on mats and runners instead of table cloths, demonstrating an Arts and Crafts sensibility.[53] Archeological finds located both inside and outside the building also indicate evidence of various purchases from local Oak Park stores.[54]

Oriental rugs were used in the home, especially on the first floor, where they were laid to appear »in chains« that were a »veritable mosaic« extending from room to room.[55] Wright favored tribal and village rugs with their colors of tan, rust and blue. Wright owned at least two books on the collecting of oriental rugs, *Rugs: Oriental and Occidental, Antique and Modern*, c. 1901, and *The Oriental Rug*, 1903.[56] The large table

in the home study featured an Uzbek susani textile. In the drafting room and its passage to the home were rugs in Native American patterns, which may have been sympathetic Arts and Crafts interpretations of Navaho originals.[57]

Wright used one reform textile from the English firm of William Morris. According to an early historic photograph, he placed portieres of an 1883 Morris woven woolen fabric, an all-over stylized leaf and flower design called Campion, at the entrance door to his octagonal architectural library. The location is significant, for intriguingly, the same fabric was one of several from the Morris firm that Henry Hobson Richardson used as portieres in his architectural library in the architectural studio attached to his home in Brookline, Massachusetts.[58]

Wright was interested in the Arts and Crafts goal of making beautiful books, and in 1896 he undertook a publishing venture with William Winslow and Chauncey Williams, for whom he had done residences in 1894 and 1895, respectively. They printed a limited edition of the Reverend William C. Gannett's essay on *The House Beautiful* illustrated with Wright's photographs and illustrations of pen-drawn figures and borders.[59] The concept of the House Beautiful had gained popularity with the publication in 1878 of Clarence Cook's book of the same name.[60] The idea continued in Chicago through the publication of the magazine *House Beautiful* started there in the winter of 1896/97.[61] This new venture's February 1897 issue carried an article on Wright's own residence, and the Oak Park studio was featured in December, 1899. Both articles were written by a Chicago architect, Alfred Granger.[62] Wright himself drew on the contrast between Arts and Crafts philosophy and the opportunities made by machine production in his own essay, »The Art and Craft of the Machine«, first given as a talk to the Chicago Arts and Crafts Society in 1901, and then delivered, rewritten, and published a number of times as a lecture and article.[63] He incorporated the design ethic he espoused in this theory in his own home and studio in the architectural details of machine-tooled flat and fillet moldings employed in woodwork and on pieces of furniture, some built by craftsmen and others at a mill using machine production methods. These pieces showed the integrity of their woods, without additional carved decorative surface enrichment.[64]

Early in his career Wright became attracted to Japanese design. Joseph Lyman Silsbee, his first employer, collected Japanese prints and was related to the most noted promotor of Japanese culture at the turn of the century, Bostonian Ernest Fenollosa.[65] After this early exposure to Japanese art and culture, Wright's knowledge of it was expanded by viewing exhibits at two World's Fairs.

Visitors were impressed with the Japanese exhibits at the World's Columbian Exposition of 1893 held in Chicago, and especially with the way the Ho-o-den, or Phoenix Pavilion, Japan's exhibit building, encompassed the traditional arts and architecture of the country. There were also Japanese goods on view and for sale in other displays at this fair. Wright also attended the Louisiana Purchase Exhibition in St. Louis in 1904 and praised its Japanese exhibit, as well as the displays of modern German and Austrian design.[66]

Wright's interest in Japanese decorative arts was shown in his home and studio. Even before his first trip to Japan in 1905 Wright used his appreciation of Japanese sources in the construction of the Oak Park building. The passageway of 1898 between the home and the studio with its wood banding and spindled stair had a Japanese architectural appearance. A large handsome Japanese blue and white dragon plate appeared in historic photographs of his architectural library published in 1899 and 1902. He owned books on Japanese topics, for example *The Floral Art of Japan* by Josiah Condor, of 1899, and *The Japanese Floral Calendar*, c. 1904.[67]

In 1905 the Wrights traveled to Japan with the Ward Willits's, collectors of Japanese prints, for whom he had designed a house in 1901. The experience was illuminating for Wright's architecture and it was the first of many trips he made to Japan. Not only did he buy prints but the couple acquired many Japanese items for their home, including black lacquerware covered soup bowls, a large tray, and a jubako (food container or picnic basket with trays), all enhanced with his signature red square, golden kesa (priest's robe) brocades, picture books, decorated paper, a long scroll painted with fish, a golden fan embellished with blue irises, and notably, a model of a Japanese house.[68] Wright took many photographs of traditional Japanese architecture and vistas and brought back purchased views of waterfalls.[69]

The impact of this trip was shown in changes made to the playroom upon his return. Wright designed new lights there in a Japanese style and also introduced small windows of Japanese character into the barrel vault of the same room.[70] He continued to draw on Japanese design sources throughout his career.

Wright's Oak Park home and studio had a critical relationship to his early career. It was not only a residence for his family, and a work place setting for his architectural practice, but it was also the scene of the struggle and process in his architectural thinking. The intriguing spaces he shifted and expanded as he designed and redesigned the building became a showcase for the artistic products of this process. From these experiments grew the architectural characteristics that distinguished his renowned Prairie School buildings: horizontal lines, overhanging roofs and balconies, ribbon windows, spaces that flow from one to another, elevated first floors with ground-hugging appearances and indirect entrances, relationship to nature and its colors, and harmony of the whole and its parts.

The home and studio's furnishings were parallel in significance. They too were the results of Wright's trials to combine function and good looks in interiors that mirrored the efforts he made with his evolving and mature Prairie architectural designs. These early pieces were minimalist in comparison to most other furnishings, machine-made in appearance, employed ideas from Arts and Crafts and Japanese aesthetic philosophies, and showed off the beauty of their material. As contemporary publications showed in their black-and-white photographs of his architecture, Wright's interiors portrayed total harmonious environments in which interior details and furnishings were carefully coordinated. This approach differed significantly in character from that being used by most other architects.

After 1909 there were more momentous, even shattering, changes in the building and the life of this family. On September 22, 1909, Wright contracted with Herman Von Holst to take over the running of his practice when he left that year for Europe with Mamah Cheney, a client's wife, to work on the celebrated Wasmuth portfolio edition of drawings of his architecture. Von Holst was a young architect who had trained at MIT and been a member of the Chicago office of Henry Hobson Richardson's successor firm of Shepley, Rutan and Coolidge before forming his own firm. He had built Arts and Crafts outbuildings for the summer estate of Chicagoan John Glessner, as well as a horizontally composed shingled summer house for Glessner's wife's family.[71]

Although Wright returned to Catherine for a short time, he moved away permanently to live with Mamah Cheney at Taliesin, the new stone home and studio he built near Spring Green, Wisconsin.[72] He never lived in the Oak Park complex again, but he reconfigured it one last time so that the home could be rented to generate an income for his family. A brick fire wall was installed to separate the home from the former studio which was reworked into a residence for his family. The first floor of the drafting room became a living room with an altered fireplace with a very low masonry mantel shelf. Wright's former architecture office became the family's dining room. Windows in this room were totally refashioned into glass double doors, side light and over door transoms that led to a new Japanese garden between the octagonal library and the home. The art glass of the new assemblage was a geometric pattern of vine leaves made from green cat's paw glass and was drawn from Japanese and Austrian influences. A kitchen was fashioned from the former connecting passage from home to studio.

There were four children's bedrooms on the squared-up second level of the floored-over drafting room. Windows in these rooms were changed to ones that had blocky areas of glass with heavy wood dividers. These were antecedents for and presaged some of the windows in Wright's Usonian clerestory designs.[73] An entirely new space for Catherine's room was built on top of the family's new dining room. The changes Wright made to his former studio to transform it into his family's living quarters included ideas then current in his work and others that anticipated new forms. Even as he exited from his work place he continued to use it to try out his architectural thinking. By 1925, Catherine lived in Chicago and Wright sold the building.[74]

As the interest in the Prairie School has grown, Wright's Oak Park home and studio has become itself the focus of study as one of the primary sites of its invention. The architect's first personal building in Illinois, along with Taliesin in Spring Green, Wisconsin, and Taliesin West in Scottsdale, Arizona, are pilgrimage sites for visitors interested in Wright's buildings and design processes. Solutions that Wright tested at the turn of the century can be noted in buildings from throughout his long and prolific career.

Many people and organizations helped in the completion of this book.

I am grateful to Hedrich-Blessing for the fine color photographs they furnished, to Michael Houlihan, President, Mark Craig and Kathleen Economou, and especially to Jon Miller for his art and craft in making them.

Additional thanks to Bruce Brooks Pfeiffer, Oscar Munoz and Penny Fowler of the Frank Lloyd Wright Foundation for use of black and white photographs and other help, to the Art Institute of Chicago for the use of a photograph, to Karen Wilson of the University of Chicago Press, Mosette Broderick and Philip Mrozinski for assistance in using other images and to Maury Bynum for the loan of a textile.

Sincere thanks to the Research Center of the Frank Lloyd Wright Foundation for the use of black and white photographs and to Angela FitzSimmons, Meg Klinkow, Cheryl A. Bachand, Erin McAffee, Jeanne Miller and Boyd Beechler in accomplishing the color work for this book and other assistance. Additional thanks to Melanie Birk and Karen Sweeney for their careful reading of the text. Joseph Fells, Seymour Persky, Lisa Schrenk, Julie Sloan and John Tucker kindly provided help with data and notes, and D. Kent Bartram, jr., put a great deal of effort into improving the technical quality of the plans.

My thanks to mentors Ross Edman, Don Kalec, John Thorpe and the late Irma Strauss as well as to the Society of Architectural Historians, owners of the Charnley-Persky House, where much of the text was written.

I am indebted to the families of Frank Lloyd Wright and Orlando Giannini for placing family objects in the home and studio building and especially to Gladys and David Wright for sharing family memories.

Special thanks to Mary Alice Molloy for her insightful editorial suggestions, to Axel Menges for his counsel and to my husband Kevin Harrington for his encouragement.

E. H.

Notes

[1] Arlene Sanderson, »House History«, *Wright Angles*, fall 1988, vol. 14, no. 4.

[2] »History of Oak Park and River Forest«, *Volunteer Manual*, Oak Park, Illinois: The Frank Lloyd Wright Home and Studio Foundation, 1993, pp. 1, 2.

[3] John Blair file, Blair Family History, The Frank Lloyd Wright Home and Studio Foundation, Research Center.

[4] Ginkgo Tree file 0211.4, Landscaping and Site Features, Research Center.

[5] »A Cottage at Tuxedo Park, N. Y., Bruce Price, Architect, 74 West 23rd Street, New York City«, *Building. A Journal of Architecture*, 18 September 1886, vol. 5, no. 12.

[6] Linda S. Phipps, »Classical Statuary and Lyrical Imagery in the Early Architecture of Frank Lloyd Wright«, (paper, Harvard University, November 1990); Research Center.

[7] Julie L. Sloan, *Light Screens: The Leaded Glass of Frank Lloyd Wright*, book in manuscript, 1994, p. 232.

[8] Stair file 0046.3, Restoration Documentation, Research Center.

[9] »View of Porch of the Above Cottage«, *Building. A Journal of Architecture*, 18 September 1886.

[10] David A. Hanks, *Decorative Designs of Frank Lloyd Wright*, New York: E. P. Dutton, 1979, pp. 54, 55.

[11] »Interpretation/Tours«, *Volunteer Manual*, p. 23.

[12] David Wright to Donald G. Kalec, 21 March 1981, Research Center.

[13] Ibid.

[14] »Interpretation/Tours«, *Volunteer Manual*, p. 24.

[15] Maginel Wright Barney, *Valley of the God Almighty Joneses*, Spring Green, Wisconsin: Unity Chapel Publications, 1965, p.133.

[16] Catherine Baxter and Lloyd Wright to Kalec, interview letter 23, June 1975, Research Center.

[17] Sloan, 1994, p. 288.

[18] Barney, *Valley*, p. 140, and *Oak Park Reporter*, 23 June 1900, p. 4; Research Center.

[19] John Lloyd Wright, *My Father Who Is Earth*, New York: G. P. Putnam's Sons, 1946, Dover edition, 1992, p. 27, Baxter and Wright to Kalec, interview letter 23, June 1975, and Maginel Wright Barney Collection, Research Center.

[20] Ann Abernathy and John G. Thorpe, *The Oak Park Home and Studio of Frank Lloyd Wright*, Oak Park, Illinois: The Frank Lloyd Home and Studio Foundation, 1993, p. 37.

[21] Charles E. White to Walter Willcox, 1903, 1904, quoted in: Lisa D.Schrenk, *An Architectural Laboratory: The Oak Park Studio of Frank Lloyd Wright*, book in manuscript, 1994.

[22] Hanks, *Decorative Designs*, pp. 2–4, 21, 22.

[23] Robert C.Twombly, *Frank Lloyd Wright. His Life and His Architecture*, New York: John Wiley and Sons, Inc., 1979, pp.16–19.

[24] Pencil sketches of FLW and CTW, Research Center, noted in: Margaret Klinkow, »A Day in the Life of Frank Lloyd Wright«, *Inland Architect*, March/April 1989, vol. 33, no. 2, p. 26, 70–71.

[25] »A Group of Upholstery Men«, *American Furniture Gazette*, April 1885, vol. 7, no. 4, after p. 20.

[26] Barney, *Valley*, p.130.

[27] Frank Lloyd Wright, *An Autobiography*, New York: Horizon, 1977, pp. 35, 52.

[28] Barney, *Valley*, pp.128, 129.

[29] Exterior Finishes file 0181.1, Restoration Documentation, Research Center.

[30] Robert Furhoff, »Home Paint Color Analysis«, 1981 to 1986 and »Studio Paint Color Analysis«, 1985, Research Center.

[31] »Interpretation/Tours«, *Volunteer Manual*, p.42.

[32] Artist files, Research Center.

[33] Conversation with David and Gladys Wright, Elaine Harrington, November 1988.

[34] Frank Lloyd Wright, *The Japanese Print: An Interpretation*, Chicago: The Ralph Fletcher Seymour Co., 1912, Horizon Press edition, 1967, p.32.

[35] *Catalog of Plaster Reproductions*, Boston: P. P. Caproni and Brother, 1911.

[36] William Allin Storrer, *Frank Lloyd Wright Companion*, Chicago: University of Chicago Press, 1993, p.36.

[37] John Lloyd Wright, *My Father*, p. 28, and White to Willcox, 1904, in: Schrenk, *Laboratory*.

[38] Frances Glessner, »I went to Field's to look at the Morris things at noon«, in: *Glessner Journal*, 27 February 1887; Chicago Historical Society, Archives.

[39] Marianna van Rensselaer, *Henry Hobson Richardson, and His Works*, Boston: Houghton, Mifflin, 1888, Prairie School Press edition, 1967, pp.134, 135.

[40] Abernathy and Thorpe, *Home and Studio*, p.17.

[41] Donald G. Kalec, »The Prairie School Furniture«, *The Prairie School Review*, Fourth Quarter, 1964, vol. 1, no. 4, pp. 5–13.

[42] Mel Byars, *The Chairs of Frank Lloyd Wright*, New York: Norfleet Press for the Preservation Press, distributed by John Wiley and Sons, forthcoming in 1996.

[43] The other print table is in the collection of the Frank Lloyd Foundation and is on view at Taliesin in Spring Green, Wisconsin, Penny Fowler to Elaine Harrington, 30 July, 1995.

[44] Hanks, *Decorative Designs*, pp. 68–70.

[45] »Interpretation/Tours«, *Volunteer Manual*, p. 22.

[46] Donald G. Kalec, »Restoring 1909 Lighting in Frank Lloyd Wright's Home and Studio«, *Architectural Lighting*, August, 1988, pp. 20–27.

[47] *Volunteer Newsletter*, The Frank Lloyd Wright Home and Studio Foundation, January, 1986, p. 11.

[48] Frank Lloyd Wright, *Autobiography*, p. 169.

[49] Wright's early use of a sink counter is documented in historic photograph RC 348 of the William G. Fricke house, designed by Wright in 1901 and photographed 1902–07, Research Center.

[50] »Interpretation/Tours«, *Volunteer Manual*, p. 37.

[51] John Lloyd Wright, *My Father*, p. 24, and Barney, *Valley*, p.134.

[52] David Wright to Carla Lind, 6 October 1983, Research Center.

[53] David Wright to Kalec, 7 June 1977, Research Center.

[54] Restoration Documentation Project, Artifact Inventory, Research Center.

[55] Alfred H. Granger, »Successful Houses«, *House Beautiful*, February 1897, vol. III, p. 66.

[56] Margaret Klinkow, *The Wright Family Library*, Oak Park, Illinois: The Frank Lloyd Wright Home and Studio Foundation Research Center, 1994, p. 7.

[57] John Lloyd Wright, *My Father*, p.34.

[58] Linda Parry, *William Morris Textiles*, New York: Viking, 1983, p.155, and Linda Parry to Elaine Harrington, c 1991, Curator's files, The Frank Lloyd Home and Studio Foundation.

[59] Mary Jane Hamilton, *Frank Lloyd and the Book Arts*, Madison, Wisconsin: Friends of the University of Wisconsin Libraries, Inc., 1993, pp. 58–61.

[60] Clarence Cook, *The House Beautiful*, New York: Scribner, Armstrong, 1878, (some of which had appeared in *Scribner's Monthly* as articles), North River Press edition, 1980, pp. 13–14.

[61] Meryle Secrest, *Frank Lloyd Wright*, New York: Alfred A. Knopf, 1992, p. 155.

[62] Granger, »Successful Houses«, *House Beautiful*, February 1897, vol. III, pp. 64–69, and »An Architect's Studio«, *House Beautiful*, December 1899, vol. VII, pp. 36–45.

[63] Frank Lloyd Wright, »Art and Craft of the Machine«, *Catalog of the Fourteenth Annual Exhibition of the Chicago Architectural Club*, Chicago: Chicago Architectural Club, 1901.

[64] John Lloyd Wright, *My Father*, p. 24.

[65] Irma Strauss, interviews, Elaine Harrington, Chicago, 1992/93, and Kevin Nute, *Frank Lloyd Wright and Japan*, New York: Van Nostrand Reinhold, 1993, pp. 22 to 25.

[66] Anthony Alofsin, *Frank Lloyd Wright. The Lost Years, 1910–1922*, Chicago: University of Chicago Press, 1993, p. 12–13.

[67] Klinkow, *Family Library*, p. 6.

[68] Twombly, *Life and Architecture*, p.113.

[69] Japan Photo Album, 1905, Research Center, described in: *Frank Lloyd Wright's Photo Album of Japan*, Rohnert Park, California: Pomegranate Art Books for Archetype Press, forthcoming in fall 1996.

[70] Marc Treib, interview, Elaine Harrington, Chicago, April 1988.

[71] A copy of the contract, supplied in 1951 by William Gray Purcell, is in the collection of the Burnham Library of the Art Institute of Chicago; in: Elaine Harrington, »International Influences on Henry Hobson Richardson's Glessner House«, *Chicago Architecture, 1872–1922, Birth of a Metropolis*, edited by John Zukowsky, Munich: Prestel–Verlag, 1987, p. 205, 207.

[72] Alofsin, *Lost Years*, p. 70, 77.

[73] Sloan, *Light Screens*, p. 304, 305.

[74] The Restoration Committee of the Frank Lloyd Wright Home and Studio Foundation, Oak Park, Illinois, *The Plan for Restoration and Adaptive Use of the Frank Lloyd Wright Home and Studio*, Chicago: The University of Chicago Press, 1978, p. 40, 42.

It should be noted that many of the following historic photographs of his home and studio are presumed to have been taken by Frank Lloyd Wright himself.

1. The home from Forest Avenue in winter, c. 1890–95. (Photographer unknown; The Frank Lloyd Wright Home and Studio Foundation)
2. Front veranda of the home, with Frank Lloyd Wright and wicker chairs. (Photographer unknown; The Frank Lloyd Wright Foundation Archives)
3. Studio entrance, c. 1898. (Photographer unknown; published in *House Beautiful*, December 1899; The Frank Lloyd Wright Home and Studio Foundation)

4. Living room showing the north wall prior to the installation of the second bay window with a Japanese brocade and an oriental rug, c.1889–95. (Photographer unknown; The Frank Lloyd Wright Foundation Archives)
5. Living room toward the inglenook with an oriental scroll, oriental rugs and the home study in the background, c. 1895–96. (Photographer unknown; The Frank Lloyd Wright Foundation Archives)
6. One of the plaster panels in the corners of the living-room ceiling, c. 1979 (Photo: Donald G. Kalec; The Frank Lloyd Wright Home and Studio Foundation)

7. Living room showing the north wall after the addition of the second bay window with a pastel by Charles Corwin and a Japanese scroll, c. 1895/96. (Photographer unknown; The Frank Lloyd Wright Foundation Archives)
8. Home study, the early dining room, with an Izbek textile on the table, seen through the living-room doorway, c. 1895/96. (Photographer unknown; The Frank Lloyd Wright Foundation Archives)

9. Later view of the dining room with three half windows in the bay, c. 1897–1902. (Photographer unknown; published in: *Ladies Home Journal*, January 1903; The Frank Lloyd Wright Home and Studio Foundation)
10. Children's playroom showing a print of Alma-Tadema's *Reading From Homer* and plaster *Winged Victory* over the door from the hall, c. 1895/96. (Photographer unknown; published in *House Beautiful*, December 1899; The Frank Lloyd Wright Home and Studio Foundation)
11. Children's playroom from the balcony with balloon shaped lamps at the ceiling, c. 1895–96. (Photographer unknown; published in: *House Beautiful*, February 1897; The Frank Lloyd Wright Home and Studio Foundation)

12. Master bedroom with gold stencils on the wall and Japanese print, c. 1893–1910. (Photographer unknown; The Frank Lloyd Wright Foundation Archives)

13. Catherine Tobin Wright's dayroom with Tobin family cradle before the central window was blocked, c. 1895/1896. (Photographer unknown; The Frank Lloyd Wright Home and Studio Foundation)

14. Studio reception hall with Teco vase found in the building during the restoration, c. 1903–07. (Photographer unknown; published in: *A Testament* by Frank Lloyd Wright, 1957; The Frank Lloyd Wright Foundation Archives)

15. Studio library with an urn by Frank Lloyd Wright and a Japanese dragon plate, c.1899. (Photographer unknown; published in: *House Beautiful*, December 1899; The Frank Lloyd Wright Home and Studio Foundation)

16. Studio library with urn, weedholder and lamp by Frank Lloyd Wright and a lamp attributed to Wright, c. 1898–1902. (Photographer unknown; published in: *Chicago Architectural Club Annual*, 1802; The Frank Lloyd Wright Home and Studio Foundation)

17. Studio library with a print table by Frank Lloyd Wright, c. 1902/03. (Photographer unknown; published in: *Architectural Record*, March 1908; The Frank Lloyd Wright Foundation Archives)

18. Studio office with Luca Della Robbia's *Boys Singing from a Book*, death mask of Ludwig van Beethoven, and urn and weedholder by Frank Lloyd Wright, c. 1898–99. (Photographer unknown; published in: *House Beautiful*, December 1899; The Frank Lloyd Wright Foundation Archives)

19. Studio office as dining room with altered window and double doors leading to a small garden, c.1911 to 1925. (Photo: Henry Fuermann; The Frank Lloyd Wright Foundation Archives)

20. Early view of the drafting room with diamond paned windows and a large sculpture of Venus, c. 1898 to 1900. (Photographer unknown; published in *The Architectural Review*, June 1900; The Frank Lloyd Wright Foundation Archives)

21. Drafting-room fireplace with plaster panel of Wright's Heller House maids and Native American patterned rugs, c. 1898/99. (Photographer unknown; The Frank Lloyd Wright Foundation Archives)

22. Drafting room as living room with altered ceiling and fireplace, c. 1911–25. (Photo: Henry Fuermann; The Frank Lloyd Wright Home and Studio Foundation)

23. Passage from the home to the studio, c. 1898 to 1910. (Photographer unknown; The Frank Lloyd Wright Foundation Archives)

24. Passage from the home to the studio as kitchen, c. 1911. (Photo: Henry Fuermann; The Frank Lloyd Wright Foundation Archives)

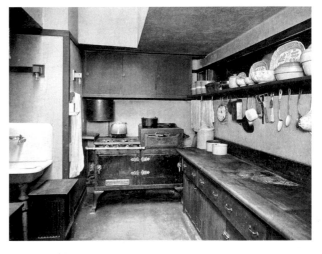

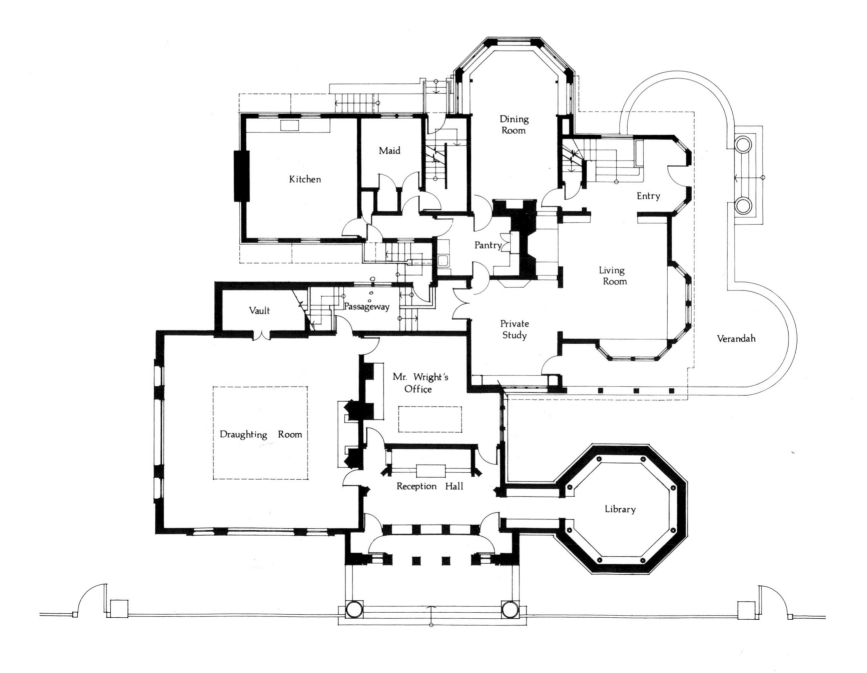

Kitchen

Maid

Dining Room

Entry

Pantry

Living Room

Vault

Passageway

Private Study

Verandah

Mr. Wright's Office

Draughting Room

Reception Hall

Library

1, 2. Home and studio, 1898. Plans of 1st and 2nd floors. (Drawings: Morgan Sweeney and Cynthia Bolsega; The Frank Lloyd Wright Home and Studio Foundation)

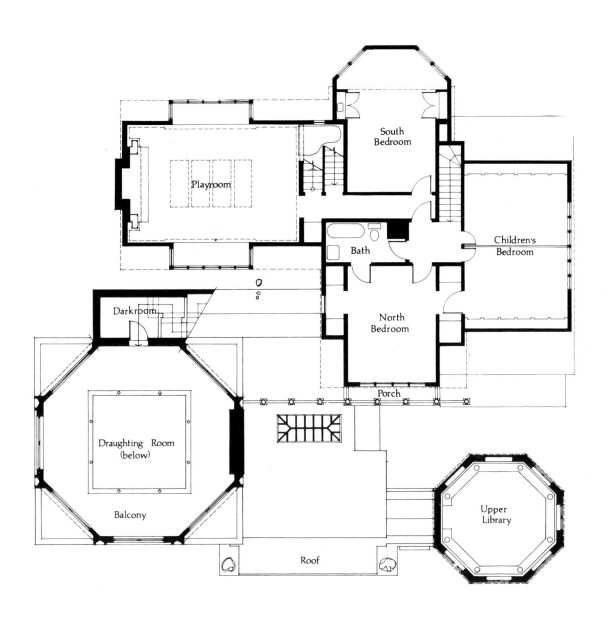

Playroom

South Bedroom

Bath

Children's Bedroom

Darkroom

North Bedroom

Draughting Room (below)

Porch

Balcony

Upper Library

Roof

0   5 m

3, 4. Home and studio, 1978. North and south elevations. (Drawings: Morgan Sweeney and Cynthia Bolsega; The Frank Lloyd Wright Home and Studio Foundation)

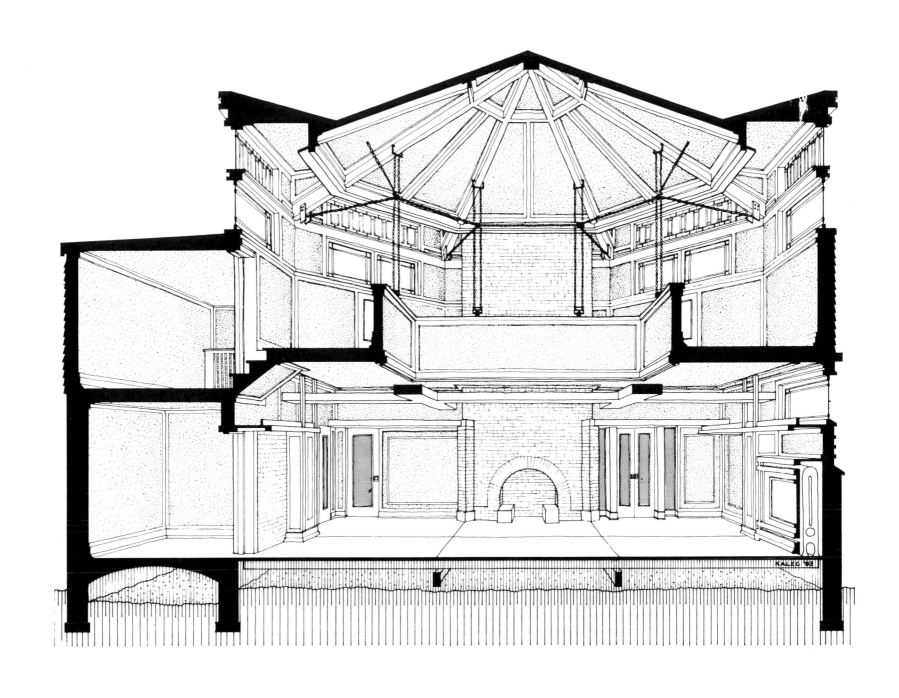

5. Drafting room, 1983. Perspective section (Drawing: Donald G. Kalec; The Frank Lloyd Wright Home and Studio Foundation)

Photographs on p. 22–56: Jon Miller,
© Hedrich-Blessing, Ltd., Chicago.

6. Forest Avenue façade.

7. Front entrance from Forest Avenue.

8. Driveway from Forest Avenue with kitchen door, playroom window and dining-room bay.

9. Exterior of the drafting room with historic ginkgo tree.

28

10. Detail of the Chicago Avenue façade with
Frank Lloyd Wright's architect's sign.
11. General view of the Chicago Avenue façade
with the studio library in the foreground.

12. Detail of the Chicago Avenue façade with the reception hall of the studio behind.
13. Studio entrance. Planters by Frank Lloyd Wright and boulder sculptures by Richard Bock.

14. Home entry hall with plaster frieze and *Venus de Milo*.
15. Arts and Crafts inglenook in the living room. Original oil painting by William Wendt.

16. Living room with armchairs and print table by Frank Lloyd Wright, original carved chest, carved taboret and pastel by Charles Corwin.

17. Home study with original black lacquerware
acquired by the Wrights on their 1905 trip to Japan.
18. Dining room. Table, chairs and high chair by
Frank Lloyd Wright.

19. Kitchen. Wall color determined by research during the restoration.

20. Pantry. The Wright's original good Limoges china is in the cupboard. Their everyday china was Blue Willow ware.

21. The low ceilinged passage
to the children's playroom.

22. Children's playroom with balcony. The width of the last two units of the barrel-vault strips are less wide than in the rest of the room, creating a perspectival illusion.

23. Children's playroom. The height of the fireplace and the low windows exaggerate the scale of the room. Prickly ash design in the ceiling fretwork. Mural of *The Fisherman and the Genie*.
24. The windows of the children's playroom relate to the grills of the Unity Temple doors. The small windows in the barrel vault and the light fixtures were added after the 1905 trip to Japan.

25. Master bedroom. First mural of a Native American by designer Orlando Giannini.

26. Roofscape of the studio office and the studio reception hall in the foreground and the studio library in the background seen from the master bedroom.

27. Master bedroom. Second mural designed by Orlando Giannini. Chair designed by Wright for his family's 1911 dining room in his altered studio wing.

28. Family bathroom. The horizontal beaded walls were reproduced from a historic photograph as part of the restoration.

29. Catherine Tobin Wright's dayroom. Tobin family cradle with oil painting by Charles Francis Browne, Catherine's instructor at the School of the Art Institute of Chicago.
30. Boys' room. Shown to represent Frank Lloyd Wright's studio from 1889 to about 1893.

31. Studio library. Floor of magnasite. Original dragon plate selected before 1905.
32. Studio reception hall. Laylights in the ceiling designed by Frank Lloyd Wright.

33. Studio reception hall with stork panels designed by Frank Lloyd Wright and executed by Richard Bock.

34. Studio office with plaster cast of Luca Della Robbia's *Boys Singing from a Book*.

35. Drafting room from the balcony. The chain harness supports the balcony and prevents the roof from pushing outward.

36. Drafting room. Later deck shelf added by Frank Lloyd Wright.